How to get rich, fall in love, lose weight, and solve all your problems by saying "NO"

by Cathy Guisewite

Andrews and McMeel, Inc.
A Universal Press Syndicate Company
Kansas City • New York

To Mickey

For many of us, it was our first word.

We shouted it through the living room,
ripping down lamps and stuffing ashtrays into
our mouths.

Mommy laughed and Daddy cheered.

It rolled out in sweet baby giggles. It danced off our fat baby feet.

Grandma cooed and baked us cookies and Grandpa pretended the flower arrangement jumped off the coffee table and got trampled all by itself.

It was fun to say "no," remember?

Then we grew up.

Saying "no" was no longer fun.

Saying "no" was no longer cheered.

Saying "no" no longer moved anyone to bake us cookies.

Until pretty soon, we couldn't even get the word out anymore.

COMPARE:

One-year-old with three-word vocabulary.

So what? Who wants to say "no" anyway? Saying "yes" is fun.

Saying "yes" makes us feel rich.

Saying "yes" makes us feel omnipotent.

Saying "yes" makes us feel so adult.

We love "yes."

The following are testimonials from people who have made "yes" a way of life and are just thrilled about it . . .

TESTIMONIAL A

It's Saturday night and here I am getting all dressed up for an eight-hour date with a man who, to my friends, I refer to as "that disgusting pig."

This is not our first date. We have now been out 36 times . . . simply because each time I go out with him I figure it will be easier to tell him I don't want to go out the next time he asks.

Not wanting to feel obligated, I have paid for 36 dinners and 36 movies.

Not wanting to feel self-conscious about speaking my mind, I have bought 36 snappy, confidence-inspiring new outfits and washed my car 36 times.

Not wanting to leave him empty-handed, I have bought gifts.

To date, I have spent $1,285.15 on that disgusting pig, all in an effort to work up the nerve to tell him I am not interested in going out with him. Tomorrow we're supposed to be getting married. Now what do I do?

Out of Control in Omaha

TESTIMONIAL B

I work in an office with 143 people. At 12:00 noon, 142 people go out to lunch and have fun. I sit at my desk and eat a soggy tuna fish sandwich from the vending machine and do all their work.

At 5:29, 142 people rush home and complain to their families about their hard day at the office. I sit at my desk, order a pizza, and do all their work.

On Saturday morning, 142 people lie in bed smiling and snoring. I sit at my desk swearing and slaving and doing all their work.

What do they know that I don't?

Frustrated in Phoenix

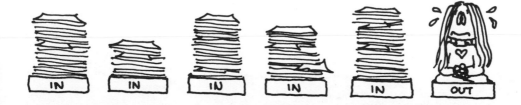

TESTIMONIAL C

Ever since I made a sizable donation to "Americans Against the Miniskirt," strange groups have been dropping over to my house unexpectedly and telling me to give them money.

Should I move or what?

Broke in Baltimore

TESTIMONIAL D

My best friend invited me to join her exclusive ladies' club and then asked if I'd be the decorating chairperson for their spring luncheon. How could I refuse?

Then my sister-in-law nominated me to receive the Outstanding Citizen Award for Nola County and then mentioned that she sure could use some help making 700 party favors for her daughter's Girl Scout troop's Halloween party.

Then my boss gave me a fabulous raise and asked if I'd mind fund-raising for his brother's political campaign.

If anything else good happens to me, I'm going to have a nervous breakdown.

Overrewarded

TESTIMONIAL E

Last Tuesday I bought a new dress for $83.95. I didn't exactly like the dress, but the sales clerk said it was adorable, and I didn't want to disappoint her.

Then she begged me to buy these hideous tangerine shoes. Well, okay, I thought, maybe they wouldn't be so bad if I dyed them.

Then she said as long as I was going to dye the shoes anyway, why not accessorize with this ugly handbag which could be dyed the same color. It took her about 20 minutes to find the handbag she was talking about and then I didn't have the heart to tell her I didn't want it.

Now she wants to go half-sies on some real estate her nephew knows about.

What do you think?

B.K.

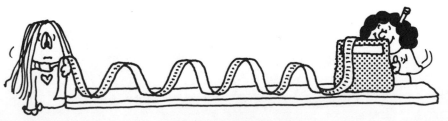

These are pathetic cases.

But we've all found ourselves in the shopping mall or in the office or in the living room or in the hall or use your imagination, Mother, agreeing to do something that wasn't exactly our idea, simply because we couldn't remember how to say "no."

We've all done it, haven't we?

It's time to consider the possibility that "yes" isn't always the most intelligent response.

Poor Reasons For Saying "Yes" To Your Date:

1. To be polite.
2. Because you're tired and if you just say "yes" you can avoid a big discussion.
3. Because you like his outfit.
4. Because it will take his mind off the fact that you're fat.
5. Because you just gave him a big speech on how liberated you are and you don't want to sound like a hypocrite.
6. Because it might be good exercise.
7. Because you're getting older and it's time you did something wacky.
8. Because you've been rejected before and you know what it feels like.
9. Because the 16-year-old in People magazine would say "yes."
10. Because you're going to write a book someday and this would be good material.

Poor Reasons For Saying "Yes" When Your Boss Gives You 37 Extra Assignments And Not One Penny Of Extra Money:

1. To get his mind off the 400 other things you haven't done yet.
2. Because everyone else in the office told him "no," and you want to endear yourself to him.
3. Because your mother always taught you to agree with people who were older than you.
4. Because you stole all the Milk Duds out of his desk.
5. Because you're dating his assistant, and you don't want him to blab it all over the office.
6. Because you took a four-hour lunch yesterday.
7. Because if you say "no," he'll launch into a big lecture about how women aren't serious about their careers.
8. Because you said "no" to the last five projects he tried to give you, and your resistance is down.
9. Because you took last week off to get your teeth cleaned.
10. Because you just accidently collated your pastrami sandwich with the company's new $92,000 copier.

Poor Reasons For Saying "Yes" When Friends And Relatives Make Outrageous Demands On Your Time And Money:

1. So everyone will be amazed by your stamina and generosity.
2. Because you've owed them a letter for six months and this will make up for it.
3. Because you said terrible things behind their backs and you're afraid they found out about them.
4. Because you want to appease your conscience for spending $200 on creme rinse last month.
5. Because they're thinner than you are.
6. Because you might meet someone cute.
7. Because it's your turn to have them over for dinner and if you contribute 80 hours of your time, you won't have to vacuum.
8. Because you want to make sure you get a Christmas present.
9. Because they might be famous someday and mention your name on television.
10. Because you just agreed to do 37 extra assignments for your boss, and now you feel guilty for ignoring your friendships.

There are many ways to say "no."
These are some of the more effective ones.

Sometimes people will catch even the most assertive of us off guard.

It is important to be prepared.

Sometimes people will demand an explanation and it will become necessary to tell a small lie.

Sometimes people will get very pushy, and it will become necessary to blame your decision on somebody else.

Sometimes you just have to hide in the closet for a while.

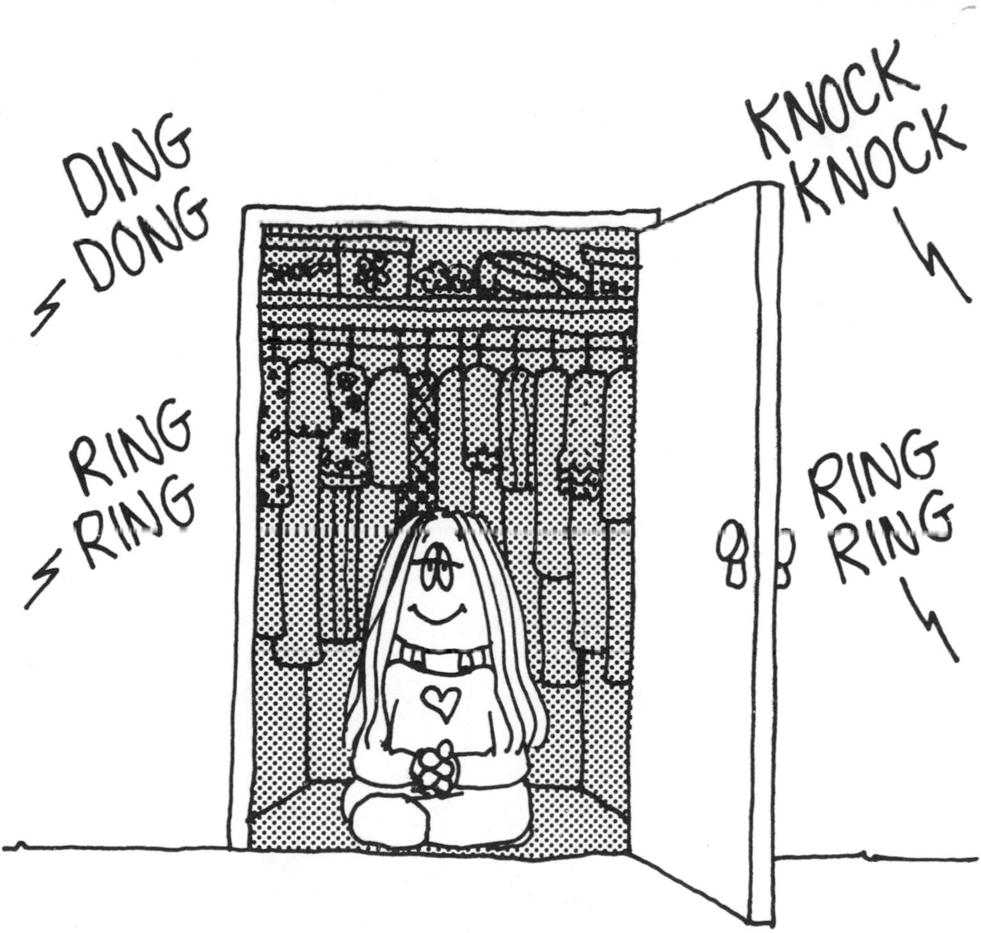
DING DONG
KNOCK KNOCK
RING RING
RING RING

Eventually, "no" will creep back into your vocabulary.

You will start to trust your own
judgment again.

The joy of being in charge of your life will overcome the guilt that others may try to make you feel.

People will secretly admire you.

Finally, you will become happy and relaxed.

You will have more energy and enthusiasm.

You will laugh and cheer and bake
yourself cookies.

With one little word, you will have reached
that blissful state of adulthood we all
strive for. . .

. . . . you'll feel just like a kid again.